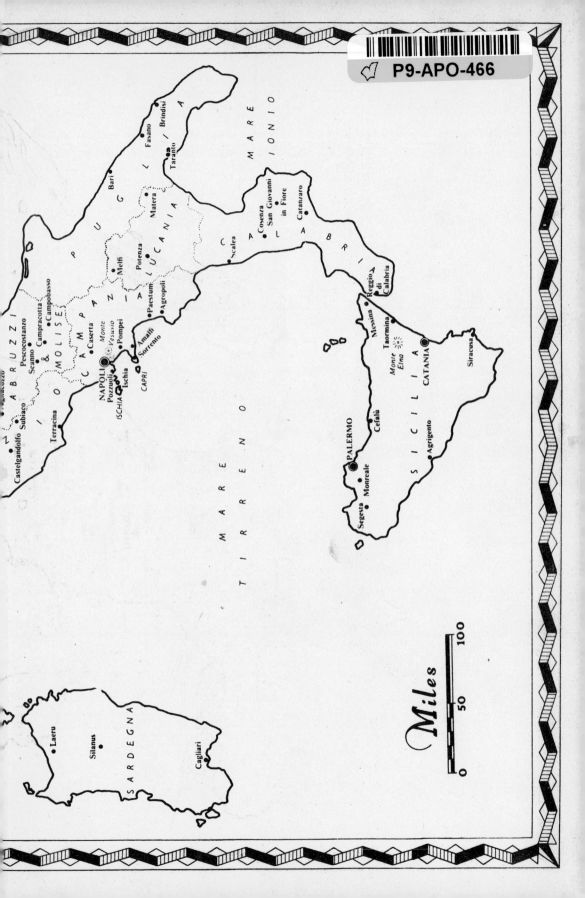

P9-APO-466

ITALY

L'ITALIE   ITALIEN

ITALY

L'ITALIE ITALIEN

A book of Photographs
with an Introduction by
RICHARD ALDINGTON

ANGLO-ITALIAN PUBLICATION

ANGLO-ITALIAN PUBLICATION LIMITED
10 ECCLESTON PLACE · LONDON SW1
Printed in Czechoslovakia

CONTENTS

INTRODUCTION
BY RICHARD ALDINGTON

PLATES

INTRODUCTION

It is a truism to say that the better we prepare ourselves before making a visit to a foreign country the more likely we are to enjoy the experience; but this is particularly true of Italy and Sicily, home of the arts and of music, where civilisations overlie one another. If the founding of Rome by refugees from fallen Troy is a myth, it gave rise to the most purely poetical of ancient epics, while the colonising of the Greeks in the south and of the Etruscans in central Italy are of course perfectly historical and have left most interesting remains. In Rome itself we are surrounded by memorials of the greatest and most durable military Empire which ever existed in Europe, and by the still-living Papacy which was its spiritual successor. Traces and influences of the Arab occupation of the South are slight, but more remains of the Normans who expelled them, and of Byzantine Greece which preceded them. Rome patiently recovered Western Europe from the invading barbarians with its apostolic armies of missionaries and monks, while Florence recovered pagan learning and re-educated the mind of intellectual Europe to a level it had lost for a thousand years. There were the great maritime republics of Pisa, Genoa and Venice, the great and opulent town of Milan, and how many smaller but vivid and individual city-states, from Perugia to Verona, from Brescia to Parma!

To this we must add the influence of Italian architects and sculptors, painters and engravers, poets and musicians. And this influence has been exerted at different epochs over a vast extent of Europe and during many centuries. The 'official art' of the Roman Empire was that of ancient Greece, adapted to the purposes of a great imperial people. The characteristic Greek art was sculpture, and in spite of the fury of wars and fanaticism and foolish greed more has survived in Italy than anywhere else. Again, at the Renaissance, Italy was the world's master in the arts, learning and literature; and it is not too much to say that almost until the end of the 19th century much of the literature of the Occident and most of its art were directly or indirectly inspired by Italy and Italian ideals.

These are interests to occupy a lifetime, and we can fully understand why for so long Italy has so greatly fascinated the cultured class of other nations. 'The grand object of travel,' said Dr. Johnson, 'is to visit the shores of the Mediterranean.' But as a matter of fact it was rather difficult to do that to any great extent in his lifetime, when the 'Grand Turk' with his fanaticism occupied so much of an area which ought to be entirely European, as it was for centuries under Rome. You needed to be wealthy, and sufficiently important to be certain of diplomatic protection, to venture into those areas, and in point of fact for most people 'the shores of the Mediterranean' meant Italy. Only rare and adventurous spirits pushed on as far as Greece, and even Sicily and southern Italy were shunned because of the very real danger of bandits.

Before the nineteenth century almost the only attraction for these wealthy pilgrims of culture was classical Italy, and particularly Naples and Rome. The limitations imposed by this taste and the fear of bandits may be judged by two episodes. A highly cultivated English traveller, after spending months in Rome and recording his 'impressions of antiquity' in detail, remarked on his way home that 'Venice afforded a few hours of surprise'. Presumably this was because the streets are canals, but Venice was not 'classical', and therefore the traveller was blind to its beauties, and not much interested in its art.

The other fact is very curious. It is stated that the three magnificent Greek temples at Paestum had been entirely forgotten by the polite world, and were 'discovered' in the eighteenth century by a party of very adventurous foreigners. This may seem improbable to those who visit them to-day with comfort and speed, either by rail or by motor-road; but conditions have entirely changed in the last two centuries. The feeble government of the 'Two Sicilies' did nothing to extirpate or even to restrain the Neapolitan Camorra, which exacted blackmail from wealthy foreigners, and was able to tip off the local bandits operating between Salerno and Paestum, or indeed anywhere in south Italy. And in that period the place was very malarious. Young ladies of that epoch setting out for Italy were supposed to thrill very agreeably (in their diaries) at the hope of seeing 'real *banditti*', but they would hardly have welcomed the reality any more than a strong chance of catching malaria.

Paestum was well protected. Even after the temples were brought into the modern tourist area the prejudice against south Italy persisted, and as recently as the 1930's the excellent motor road south from Naples ended at Paestum, or rather was prolonged only by a far less excellent road. In earlier days, and well into the nineteenth century, Italy south of Salerno and the island of Sicily could be visited by foreigners only under armed escort.

The many interests of Italy — even limited to the area from the Alps to the Bay of Naples —meant that there was a constantly-renewed cosmopolitan society in the big towns, particularly in Rome. And they also meant that, at any rate up till the war of 1939, Italy sheltered many quiet foreigners who were studying some subject of Italian history or literature or art, and were happy to pass their lives in this way, writing books or painting pictures or merely devoting themselves to the happiness of living in so beautiful a country. Many books or parts of books have been written about the famous people who have lived or stayed in Italy, but it is a pity that nobody in the last century seems to have thought of recording the humbler guests whose stay, at the best, is recorded only by a few oil paintings fading on the walls of a little *pension* or by a forgotten travel book. Or, still less flatteringly, by a volume of verse which nobody ever read.

Italy and the succeeding Italian governments have long been aware of their responsibilities as guardians of the picturesque towns and innumerable works of art of all kinds inherited from a past so long and so fertile. As in Spain, religion has been a protection, and the cathedrals and many churches are museums of sculpture and painting as well as sacred places. They are truly the art treasuries of the poor, who otherwise would never see such things. And the state of preservation is usually good—there have been no puritan or political destructions such as occurred in England and France, and none of the facetious vandalism which chops pieces off statues and inscribes initials in marble. Yet there used to be considerable criticism of Italian guardianship of its own inheritance, in spite of the fact that large sums were spent in upkeep and protection. The recent war, which carried demolition and destruction from one end of Italy to the other, has to some extent lightened the burden of responsibility without appreciably diminishing the total effect.

Obviously a large and energetic modern people cannot all live in historical monuments. There are indeed such masterpieces of Renaissance art as Pienza, the birthplace of Pius II, and of Baroque architecture as Lecce in Puglia, but it would be absurd to expect that all Italy could be so preserved. Great modern cities such as Milan, Genoa, Naples and Rome itself have enormously increased in population, and consequently have whole quarters of new buildings. Parts of modern Genoa have quite an American look. Nor need we regret this, as long as the beautiful older quarters and buildings are protected. There was no more enthusiastic, one might say fanatical, lover of medieval Italy and its art than the English critic, John Ruskin. Yet it is related of him, amusingly if not truly, that after spending weeks of careful art-study in ancient hill towns such as Assisi, Perugia, Gubbio, Montepulciano, and so forth, he would suddenly stop, take the express to a big modern town like Milan or Turin, put on evening dress and dine at a fashionable restaurant and then go to the theatre or opera. After which he would return to his Giottos and Peruginos. The lesson is salutary. However refreshing and stimulating we may find an escape from the tumultuous present to the serenity of the past, we can't live in it.

When we come to look at modern Italy in detail we find it divided for administrative purposes into provinces, some of which bear the names of ancient city-states or duchies: but it is well to remember that they do not necessarily cover the same areas, while some once-important duchies such as those of Milan, Ferrara, Mantua, and even Urbino now name only the parent town. Modern united Italy is less than a century old, a thing of yesterday in the annals of so ancient a country. Not until the defeat of France in the Franco-Prussian war of 1870 did Rome become the capital of the then Italian monarchy, which added the States of the Church to its dominions. Before 1914 many in Rome, natives as well as foreigners, deplored the change of the spiritual capital of a world religion into that of a modern kingdom — now a republic. But what other possible capital was there, in spite of the wealth and commercial splendour of Milan and the fact that for a time it had been the capital of the Roman Empire?

A result of this recent unification is that the local patriotism and peculiarities of age-old city-states still persist, and historical memory is keen. I had an amusing little example of this in the 1930's when driving in Sicily in a car with the licence-plate of Florence. On more than one occasion we were suddenly greeted with a shout of 'Palle! Palle!' which was the old rallying-cry of the Medici faction, and disappeared with Gian Gastone in the eighteenth century. I thought it was done in derision, but my Italian friend said No, it was a home-sick Florentine. Indeed the people from the wealthier northern parts of Italy did in those days complain bitterly of the discomforts and what they were pleased to call 'the barbarism' of the South, and longed to be back in the comfort and plenty of their home towns. All this is changing rapidly, but the old differences remain at least among the people; and nobody who has lived in Italy is likely to mistake a Venetian for a Florentine or a Genoese for a Roman. In their own eyes the Roman people are still the 'Roman people' or 'the Romans'; and what the rest of the world would call 'Romans' they gravely call 'the *ancient* Romans'. The sense of continuity and pride is impressive, and there are even contentions between the two banks of the Tiber as to which is truly 'Roman'.

With all this local pride and prejudice there seems to be none of the separatism which exists in the British Isles, and to some extent in Alsace, Brittany and even, platonically, in Provence. All sensible Italians are convinced of the necessity and benefit of their unity (and so, as a matter of fact, are all sensible Frenchmen) but they leave the old ways with regret. Read the resounding thousand-years roll-call of the Doges of Venice, and ask yourself if you can feel the same thrill for some representative, however amiable and patriotic, of the Department of the Interior!

In spite of the important, indeed decisive, part played by Cavour and the Piedmontese in the liberation and unifying of Italy, Piedmont seems one of the least Italian provinces. Apart from the city of Turin, which until 1860 was the capital of the kingdom of Sardinia, the attraction of the province lies largely in the sub-Alpine scenery, especially in the beautiful Val d'Aosta, and the mountain fastnesses. The neighbouring province of Lombardy brings us at once into historical Italy, containing as it does the great ducal cities of Milan and Mantua (sites of Virgil's birthplace and d'Annunzio's last home) and the lakes of Como, Maggiore, Garda and Iseo. No visitor to Italy cares to miss Milan's vast and ornate cathedral, one of the finest as well as largest in the world, or the great fortress-palace of the Sforzas, or the church of St. Ambrogio, or Leonardo's 'Last Supper'... As a personal choice I would add Pavia, and in its vicinity the great Carthusian monastery with its superb Renaissance workmanship, ranging from the Cloisters to the empty tomb of Lodovico. Then Mantua with its fascinating ducal palace, the Palazzo del Té, and the church where Mantegna lies... Giulio Romano worked long at the palace, and produced strange frescoes of giants, and there are portraits of favourite race-horses. But if one starts remembering Italy in detail there is no end to it.

Proud Venice still gives her name to the province of Venezia—in the days when they flew the banner of San Marco outside the cathedral (perhaps they still do) one didn't much look at the red, white and green tricolour. What is there to be said of Venice in a paragraph? 'O for one hour of blind old Dandolo'? That Bellini portrait of Lorenzo Loredan in London? Or a snatch from an old *Punch* poem which unexpectedly starts up from a nook of memory?

> With all respect to old R. B.,
> My own especial spring-time prayer
> Is 'O to be in Italy,
> In Venice, now that April's there.'

Yet six weeks is above the limit of a stay in Venice. After that one longs for 'green haunts and loneliness', and marvels that people can spend their lives in sky, water and Istrian stone. But near at hand are Padua, Vicenza, Verona... In a privately-owned villa outside Vicenza are some superb Tiepolo frescoes—when I was granted the privilege of seeing them I wondered that a copy of James Joyce's *Ulysses* was left in the *salone!*

Modern Emilia brings together Bologna *la grassa*, ducal Ferrara with its memories of Ariosto and Tasso, Parma and Correggio, Modena, Rimini—where they destroyed the temple of Malatesta—and Ravenna of the basilicas and matchless Greek mosaics, where Dante died and Byron lost a super-purloined heart. Theodoric the Ostrogoth and Galla Placidia are also remembered here...

Tuscany, it is the heart and soul of poetic Italy—what a chaos of happy memories surges up at the mere name 'Florence', and there are Siena, Pienza, San Gimignano, Pistoia, Prato, Lucca, Pisa. The poetic imagination of these Tuscans! How well I remember driving my regretted friend Orioli to Prato to buy what he assured me was the most exquisite veal in the world—only to come on a gigantic ox carcase hewn in half by some Cyclops and labelled 'Vitello Giovanissimo'—new-born calf! Who could fail to love a people whose imagination so embellishes life? See how the Tuscan—or Etruscan —imagination has embellished Florence itself, and respect the Spirito del Cupolano. I think of days, literally days, spent in Siena cathedral, 'working out' the many ancient symbols carved in hidden nooks of the great nave with its frieze of Papal busts; which nave, but for the Black Death, would have been the mere transept of the vast cathedral imagined and actually begun. And Lucca, and Pisa.

And still we are not halfway through Italy. Stands the palace of Urbino where it did? Is there still that delicious muscatel wine at San Marino? What of Borgo San Sepolcro, and those Piero della Francesca paintings—and Arezzo? Orvieto—how wonderful to get away from the *fiaschetti* sold on the railway platform, hunt about, and finally descending some six or seven steps into a wine-shop of antiquity, to find cool draughts of the right Orvieto white wine! A fitting pendant to the façade of the Cathedral and the Signorelli chapel, not to mention the vast well from which the Popes (with that wine at hand) drew water, doubtless to mortify the flesh. Appropriately, they used donkeys to bring up the water.

In spite of changed views of life and art, and lacerations due to what is called 'Progress', Rome still remains the foremost attraction of Italy. As the enthusiastic but not very eloquent admirer put it: 'Venice is Venice, but Rome's *Rome*.' One sees what he meant! There are said to be about five hundred churches in Rome, most of which have something, many of which have a great deal, worth study. The Vatican and its miles of galleries of sculpture, the museums, the Roman Forum, the Tiber bridges, the catacombs, the mosaics... they are inexhaustible. There is one of those invented but symbolically true anecdotes about one of the Popes giving audience to some distinguished foreigners who had just arrived, and asking each in turn how long he meant to stay. 'Three days,' said one. 'Ah,' said the Pope, 'you'll see everything in Rome.' 'Three months,' said the second. 'You'll see a lot of Rome.' 'Three years,' said the third. 'You'll begin to know Rome!'

Of course, there will always be those who prefer the Bay of Naples, less for the sake of Naples itself than for the islands, for the buried Roman towns of Pompeii and Herculaneum, and the views and towns along 'the Amalfi drive'—Castellammare, Sorrento, Positano, Ravello and Amalfi itself. The area contains some of the most beautiful sea-coast scenery in Europe, matched only by that on either side of the Straits of Messina, best seen perhaps from Taormina. Adventurous souls who don't mind roughing it should try the peaks and valleys of the Abruzzi and the comparatively unfrequented parts of the old kingdom of Naples south of Paestum. And after that there are still Sicily and Sardinia to explore!

The old Neapolitan proverb used to say, rather threateningly, 'See Naples and die.' It seems a harsh penalty for admiring a beautiful place. Perhaps we could adapt it to our own times and say, 'See Italy, and come back and see some more of it!'

R. A.

INTRODUCTION

C'est une vérité bien connue que l'on jouit mieux d'un voyage si l'on s'y est préparé longtemps à l'avance. Ceci est d'autant plus vrai pour l'Italie et la Sicile, mère-patrie des arts et de la musique, où plusieurs civilisations se sont succédées. Si la fondation de Rome par des réfugiés de Troie vaincue est un mythe, celui-ci a donné naissance au plus poétique des poèmes épiques de l'antiquité; tandis que la colonisation par les Grecs dans le sud et par les Étrusques dans l'Italie centrale est parfaitement historique et a laissé des vestiges importants. À Rome nous sommes environnés par les souvenirs de l'Empire militaire le plus grand et le plus durable qui ait jamais existé en Europe, et par une Papauté toujours vivante qui est son successeur spirituel. Les traces et l'influence de l'occupation arabe du sud sont peu importantes, mais on retrouve plus de restes des Normands qui les expulsèrent et de la Grèce byzantine qui les précéda.

Rome regagna patiemment l'Europe occidentale de l'invasion barbare avec ses armées apostoliques de moines et de missionnaires, tandis que Florence retrouvait la culture païenne et relevait l'esprit intellectuel de l'Europe à un niveau qu'il avait perdu depuis mille ans. Il y avait les grandes Républiques maritimes de Pise, Gênes et Venise, la grande ville opulente de Milan, et combien de cités plus petites mais vivantes et uniques, depuis Pérouse jusqu'à Vérone, de Brescia à Parme!

À ceci il faut ajouter l'influence des architectes, sculpteurs, peintres, graveurs, poètes et musiciens italiens. Cette influence a été exercée à diverses époques sur une vaste étendue de l'Europe et pendant plusieurs siècles. L'art «officiel» de l'Empire romain était celui de la Grèce antique adapté aux intérêts du grand peuple impérial. L'art typique de la Grèce était la sculpture, et malgré la furie des guerres, du fanatisme et de la sotte cupidité, plus de statues ont survécu en Italie que partout ailleurs. De plus, pendant la Renaissance, l'Italie dominait le monde de l'art, de la culture et de la littérature; et ce n'est nullement une exagération de dire que la plupart de la littérature et de l'art occidentaux étaient plus ou moins directement inspirés par l'Italie et par l'idéal italien.

Il y a là toute une vie d'intérêt, et on comprend pourquoi depuis si longtemps l'Italie a tellement fasciné les érudits des autres pays. Le Docteur Johnson a dit: «Le grand but du voyage est de visiter les rives de la Méditerranée». Mais à vrai dire c'était assez difficile à faire de son temps quand le «grand Turc», avec son fanatisme, occupait une partie substantielle du territoire qui aurait dû être entièrement européen comme il le fut pendant des siècles sous Rome. Il fallait être riche et suffisamment important pour être assuré d'une protection diplomatique si l'on voulait s'aventurer dans ces pays; et pour la plupart des gens «les rives de la Méditerranée» signifiaient l'Italie. Seuls de rares esprits aventureux poussaient jusqu'à la Grèce, et même la Sicile et l'Italie du sud étaient évitées à cause du réel danger des bandits. Avant le 19e siècle l'Italie classique, en particulier Naples et Rome, était seule à attirer ces riches pèlerins de la culture. Deux épisodes nous démontrent les limites imposées par ce goût et par la peur des bandits. Un voyageur anglais, ayant passé plusieurs mois à Rome, remarqua pendant son voyage de retour que «Venise procurait quelques heures de surprise». Sans doute parce que les rues étaient des canaux, mais Venise n'était pas «classique», donc le voyageur restait aveugle devant ses beautés et peu intéressé par son art. L'autre épisode est très curieuse. Il paraît que les trois magnifiques temples grecs à Paestum avaient été complètement oubliés par le haut monde et furent «découverts» au 18e siècle par un groupe très audacieux d'étrangers.

Cela peut paraître invraisemblable à tous ceux qui les visitent aujourd'hui avec confort et vitesse, en voiture ou par train, mais les conditions ont totalement changé pendant les deux derniers siècles. Le faible gouvernement des Deux Siciles ne fit rien pour supprimer ou même freiner la Camorra Napolitaine qui faisait chanter les riches étrangers, et qui renseignait les bandits locaux qui opéraient entre Salerne et Paestum, ainsi que dans toute l'Italie du sud. Et à l'époque l'endroit était très paludéen. Les jeunes filles de ce temps-là, qui partaient pour l'Italie, étaient sensées de se rejouir à l'idée de rencontrer de «vrais banditti», mais en réalité elles auraient à peine accueilli une telle rencontre avec plus de joie que la forte chance qu'elles avaient d'attraper le paludisme. Paestum était bien protégé! Même lorsque les temples furent portés à la connaissance des touristes modernes, le préjugé contre l'Italie du sud persistait. Même vers 1930 l'excellente autostrade de Naples se terminait à Paestum, et continuait comme une route ordinaire. Au 19e siècle l'Italie au sud de Salerne et la Sicile ne pouvaient être visité (en général) que par des touristes accompagnés d'une escorte armée.

Les nombreux intérêts de l'Italie, même limitée à l'étendue entre les Alpes et la Baie de Naples, faisaient venir une société cosmopolite constamment renouvelée aux grandes villes, surtout à Rome. Et puis, tout au moins jusqu'à la guerre de 1939, l'Italie abritait beaucoup d'étrangers qui étudiaient quelque sujet de l'histoire ou de la littérature ou de l'art italiens, et qui étaient heureux de passer leur vie à écrire ou à peindre ou à se dévouer tout simplement à la joie de vivre dans un pays tellement beau. Bien des livres ont été écrits sur les gens illustres qui ont habité ou ont résidé un moment en Italie, mais il est dommage que personne n'ait songé au siècle dernier à mentionner les hôtes plus modestes dont le séjour est au plus consigné à quelques peintures à l'huile passant au soleil sur les murs d'une petite pension, ou par quelque livre de voyages oublié, ou encore d'une façon moins flatteuse par un recueil de poésies que personne n'a jamais lu.

L'Italie et les gouvernements italiens successifs ont longtemps été conscients de leurs responsabilités en tant que gardiens de villes pittoresques et d'oeuvres d'art de toutes sortes héritées d'un passé si ancien et si riche. Ainsi qu'en Espagne la religion a joué le rôle de protectrice, et bien des cathédrales et des églises, tout en étant des lieux sacrés, sont des musées de sculpture et de peinture. Ce sont vraiment des sanctuaires d'art pour les pauvres qui sans cela ne verraient jamais de telles choses. L'état de conservation est bon en général; il n'y a pas eu de destruction politique ou puritaine comme en France et en Angleterre, ni ce vandalisme facétieux qui défigure les statues et grave des initiales sur le marbre. Cependant on critiquait fort les soins pris par l'Italie de son propre héritage, malgré les sommes importantes dépensées pour sa protection et son entretien. La dernière guerre qui porta la destruction d'un bout à l'autre de l'Italie a allégé en partie le poids de cette responsabilité, sans toutefois en diminuer l'effet total.

Il est évident qu'une grande population énergique et moderne ne peut vivre entièrement dans des monuments historiques. Certes, il y a des chefs-d'oeuvre d'art de la Renaissance tels que Pienza (lieu de naissance de Pie II) et d'architecture baroque comme Lecce dans les Pouilles; mais il serait absurde de penser que toute l'Italie puisse être ainsi conservée. La population des grandes villes telles que Gênes, Naples et Rome elle-même, s'est énormément augmentée, et en conséquence des quartiers entiers de constructions modernes se sont formés. Certaines parties de Gênes ont un aspect américain. Cependant nous ne devons pas le regretter tant que les vieux quartiers et leurs beaux palaces sont préservés.

Il n'y a pas d'admirateur plus enthousiaste — on pourrait presque dire fanatique — de l'Italie du moyen âge que l'écrivain anglais, John Ruskin. L'histoire que l'on raconte à son sujet est amusante si non vraie. Après avoir passé des semaines à étudier soigneusement l'art des vieilles villes perchées sur des collines, comme Assise, Pérouse, Gubbio, Montepulciano, il s'arrêtait soudain, prenait le train pour une grande ville moderne telle que Milan ou Turin, se mettait en habit, et dînait dans un restaurant en vogue pour aller ensuite au théâtre ou à l'opéra. Puis il retournait à ses Giotto et à ses Perugino. La leçon est salutaire. Aussi rafraîchissante et stimulante que nous puissions trouver une évasion du tumulte des temps modernes pour la sérénité du passé, nous ne pouvons y vivre.

Lorsque nous observons en détail l'Italie moderne nous la trouvons divisée en provinces pour des raisons d'administration parmi lesquelles certaines portent le nom d'anciens Villes-États ou Duchés. Mais il est bon de rappeler qu'elles ne couvrent pas forcément la même superficie et que des Duchés jadis importants comme Milan, Ferrare, Mantoue et même Urbin, ne conservent plus que les noms des villes mères. L'Italie unie d'aujourd'hui ne date pas d'un siècle, un événement d'hier dans les annales d'un si vieux pays. Ce ne fut qu'après la défaite de la France dans la guerre contre la Prusse en 1870 que Rome devint la capitale du Royaume d'Italie, ce qui ajouta les États de l'Église à ses possessions. Avant 1914 à Rome bien des gens, étrangers comme italiens, regrettaient le changement survenu dans cette capitale spirituelle d'une religion mondiale, devenue capitale d'un État moderne. Mais quelle autre capitale possible y-avait-il, malgré la richesse et la magnificence commerciale de Milan et le fait que cette dernière avait été pendant quelque temps la capitale de l'Empire romain?

Un résultat de cette unification récente est que le patriotisme local et les particularités des anciennes Villes-États existent toujours, et que la mémoire historique du peuple est vive. J'en eus un amusant petit exemple en 1930 alors que je traversais la Sicile en voiture avec une plaque d'immatriculation florentine. Plus d'une fois nous fûmes accueillis par le cri: «Palle, Palle!» qui était le vieux cri de ralliement des Medicis, et qui disparut avec Gian Gastone au 18e siècle. Je pensais que ce cri était pour se moquer de nous, mais mon ami italien m'assura du contraire; c'était quelque Florentin qui avait le mal du pays. En effet les habitants des endroits prospères de l'Italie du nord se plaignaient amèrement des désagréments et de ce qu'ils aimaient appeler «le barbarisme» du sud, soupirant après le confort et l'aisance de leurs villes. Tout cela est en rapide transformation, mais les anciennes particularités existent toujours, et il n'y a personne qui ait habité en Italie capable de confondre un Vénétien avec un Florentin ou un Gênois avec un Romain. À ses yeux le peuple romain est toujours le «Populus Romanus» ou «les Romains», et ce que le reste du monde appelle les Romains, eux les appellent sérieusement «les anciens Romains». Ces sentiments de continuité et de fierté sont impressionnants, et il y a même opposition entre les deux rives du Tibre. Lequel des deux est-il vraiment «Romain»?

Avec tous ces préjugés et cette fierté locale il ne semble pas y avoir le séparatisme qui existe dans les Iles Britanniques et à un certain point en Alsace, en Bretagne, et même de façon platonique en Provence. Tous les Italiens sensés sont convaincus de la nécessité et de l'avantage de leur unité (et, à vrai dire, tous les Français aussi) mais ils abandonnent leurs vieilles habitudes avec regret. Lisez, par exemple, la liste longue et impressionnante des Doges de Venise, et dîtes-moi si on peut ressentir autant d'émotion pour les Préfets, quoique aimables et patriotiques, envoyés par le Ministère de l'Intérieur.

Malgré le rôle important, même décisif, de Cavour et des Piémontais dans la libération et l'unification de l'Italie, le Piémont nous semble une des provinces les moins italiennes. A part la ville de Turin qui jusqu'en 1860 fut la capitale du royaume de Sardaigne, l'attrait de cette province réside plus particulièrement dans le paysage prèalpin, surtout dans la beauté du Val d'Aoste et des montagnes. La province avoisinante, la Lombardie, nous transporte d'un coup dans l'Italie historique avec les grandes villes des Duchés de Milan et de Mantoue, lieux d'association littéraire, pays natal de Virgile, et la dernière demeure d'Annunzio, les lacs aussi de Côme, Majeur, Garde et Iseo. Aucun touriste ne passerait sans voir l'immense Cathédrale richement ornée de Milan, parmi les plus belles et plus grandes du monde, ou le palais de Sforza, la galerie de Poldo-Pezzoli, l'église de Sant' Ambrogio, et la Cène de Léonard de Vinci... Personnellement j'y ajouterais Pavie, et à proximité la Chartreuse de Pavie dont le style renaissance est magnifique, depuis le cloître jusqu'au tombeau vide de Lodovico. Puis, à Mantoue il y a un palais ducal fascinant, avec le Palazzo del Té, et l'église où repose Mantegna... Giulio Romano travailla longtemps à ce palais, et y produisit d'étranges fresques de géants; et il y aussi des portraits de chevaux de course favoris!

Mais si on commence à se remémorer l'Italie en détail on n'en finira plus.

Venise la fière donne toujours son nom à la province de Venise. Les jours où la bannière de St. Marc flottait devant la cathédrale on ne voyait guère le tricolore rouge, blanc et vert. Que peut-on dire de Venise dans un paragraphe? «O for one hour of blind old Dandolo»? (Byron) («O seulement une heure de Dandolo aveuglé»). Ce portrait de Lorenzo Loredan fait par Bellini que l'on peut voir à Londres? Ou ce bref extrait d'un vieux «Punch» qui surgit à l'improviste à la mémoire:

> With all respect to old R. B.,
> My own especial spring-time prayer
> Is 'O to be in Italy,
> In Venice, now that April's there.'*

Cependant la limite d'une visite à Venise est d'environ six semaines. Ensuite on aspire aux «refuges verdoyants et à la solitude», et on s'étonne que des gens puissent passer leur vie entre l'eau, le ciel et la pierre d'Istrie. Mais non loin il y a Padoue, Vicence, Vérone... Près de Vicence, dans une villa privée, il y a quelques fresques superbes de Tiepolo. Quand j'eus le privilège de les voir je m'étonnai d'apercevoir dans le salon un exemplaire de l'Ulysse de James Joyce. Cela détonnait!

L'Émilie moderne rassemble Bologne «la grassa», la ville ducale de Ferrare avec ses souvenirs d'Arioste et de Tasse, Parme et Correggio, Modène, Rimini, où ils ont détruit le temple de Malatesta, et Ravenne avec ses basiliques et ses incomparables mosaïques, où mourut Dante et où Byron perdit un coeur déjà tant de fois volé! Là aussi on se souvient de Theodoricus l'Ostrogoth et de Galla Placida...

La Toscane, c'est le coeur et l'âme de l'Italie poétique. Combien de souvenirs heureux surgissent à la moindre évocation de Florence — et puis, il y a Sienne, Pienza, San Gimignano, Pistoia, Prato, Lucques, Pise. Ah! l'imagination poétique de ces Toscans! Que je me souviens bien du jour où j'allais

---

* Je plagie Robert Browning mais avec respect en chantant ma propre prière de printemps: Oh, être maintenant en Italie, à Venise, puisque c'est Avril!

à Prato avec mon regretté ami Orioli afin d'acheter ce qu'il m'assurait être le veau le plus exquis du monde, pour me trouver devant la plus gigantesque carcasse de bœuf coupé en deux par quelque Cyclops et portant l'étiquette «Vitello Giovanissimo» — veau nouveau né! Comment ne pas aimer un peuple dont l'imagination embellit la vie d'une telle façon? Voyez comment l'imagination toscane ou étrusque a embelli la ville de Florence elle-même, et respectez le «spirito del Cupolano»! Je pense aux jours entiers passés dans la cathédrale de Sienne à découvrir les nombreux symboles anciens gravés dans les recoins cachés de la grande nef avec sa frise de bustes de Papes. Cette nef, sans la Grande Peste ne serait que le transept de la vaste cathédrale dont on rêvait. Et Lucques, et Pise!

Et nous n'avons pas vu la moitié de l'Italie. Le palais d'Urbin est-il encore debout? A St Marin trouve-t-on toujours de ce délicieux vin muscat? Et Borgo San Sepolcro? Et les tableaux de Piero della Francesca? Et Arezzo? Orvieto! Quel bonheur d'échapper aux «fiaschetti» que l'on vend sur les quais des gares et, tout en flânant dans les rues, descendre six ou sept marches et trouver enfin dans une cave de l'antiquité le vrai vin blanc d'Orvieto! On ne peut trouver mieux comme pendant à la façade de la cathédrale et à la chapelle Signorelli, sans parler de ce grand puits où les Papes (avec ce vin à portée de la main) tiraient de l'eau, sans doute pour la mortification de la chair. A juste titre ils se servaient d'ânes pour porter l'eau.

Malgré les différentes conceptions de la vie et de l'art et les changements dûs à ce qui s'appelle le «Progrès», Rome est toujours le centre d'attraction de l'Italie. Comme s'écria un admirateur enthousiaste mais peu éloquent: «Venise est Venise, mais Rome c'est *Rome!*» On comprend ce qu'il voulait dire. Il y a, paraît-il, environ cinq cents églises dans Rome, dont la plupart valent la peine d'être étudiées. Le Vatican et ses kilomètres de galeries de sculpture, les musées, le Forum, les ponts du Tibre, les catacombes, les mosaïques… c'est inépuisable. Il y a une anecdote fantaisiste mais dont la morale n'en est pas moins vraie, qui raconte une audience qu'eurent avec le Pape quelques étrangers influents qui venaient d'arriver. Leur parlant chacun à leur tour le Pape demanda combien de temps ils avaient l'intention de rester. «Trois jours», répondit le premier. «Ah,» dit le Pape, «vous pourrez tout voir dans Rome.» «Trois mois,» répondit le second. «Vous verrez une bonne partie de Rome.» «Trois ans,» dit le troisième. «Vous commencerez à connaître Rome.»

Sans doute il y aura toujours ceux qui préféreront la Baie de Naples, non pour la ville elle-même mais pour les îles, pour les restes romains de Pompéi et d'Herculaneum, les sites et les villes le long de la «corniche Amalfi», Castellammare, Positano, Sorrente, Ravello et Amalfi, où on peut voir une des plus belles côtes d'Europe qui n'a son égal qu'en les deux côtes longeant le détroit de Messine, peut-être le plus avantageusement de Taormina. Les âmes d'aventuriers dédaigneux des obstacles devraient essayer les sommets et les vallées des Abruzzes, et les endroits moins fréquentés de l'ancien royaume de Naples au sud de Paestum. Et il nous reste encore à explorer la Sicile et la Sardaigne!

Le vieux proverbe napolitain affirme d'une façon un peu menaçante: «Voir Naples et mourir». C'est une punition assez dure pour avoir admiré la beauté du pays. On pourrait peut-être l'adapter à notre époque et dire: «Voir l'Italie, aller la revoir.»

R. A.

EINLEITUNG

Es ist allgemein bekannt, daß man einen Besuch im Ausland um so mehr genießt, je besser man sich darauf vorbereitet hat. Dies ist, soweit Italien und Sizilien – diese Sitze der Kunst und der Musik — in Betracht kommen, besonders wahr, da hier verschiedene Zivilisationsschichten erkennbar sind. Wenn es auch nur eine Sage ist, daß Rom von Flüchtlingen aus dem gefallenen Troja gegründet wurde, so entsprang doch das poetischste klassische Heldengedicht aus dieser Sage; die Kolonisation der Griechen in Süditalien und der Etrusker in Mittelitalien sind hingegen historisch völlig bewiesen, und hochinteressante Nachlasse sind gefunden worden.

In Rom sind wir von den Denkmälern des größten und dauerhaftesten kriegerischen Kaiserreichs, das es je in Europa gegeben hat, umgeben, wie auch von seinem geistigen Nachfolger, dem Papsttum, das heute noch weiterlebt. Spuren und Einfluß der arabischen Besetzung Süditaliens gibt es kaum, aber von den Normannen, die die Araber vertrieben, und von den byzantinischen Griechen, die ihnen vorausgingen, ist mehr geblieben. Mit Geduld eroberte Rom, mit seinen apostolischen, aus Missionaren und Mönchen bestehenden Armeen, Westeuropa aus den Händen des barbarischen Überfalls wieder, während Florenz das vorchristliche Wissen wiederentdeckte und den intellektuellen Geist Europas wieder zu einer Höhe erzog, die er seit tausend Jahren verloren hatte. Da gab es die großen Seerepubliken: Pisa, Genua und Venedig, das große reiche Mailand und noch viele kleinere, aber lebhafte und charaktervolle Freistädte, von Perugia bis Verona, von Brescia bis Parma.

Zu all diesem kommt noch der Einfluß italienischer Baumeister und Bildhauer, Maler und Kupferstecher, Dichter und Musiker. Dieser Einfluß machte sich zu verschiedenen Zeiten und durch viele Jahrhunderte hindurch in einem großen Teil Europas geltend. Die „offizielle Kunst" des romanischen Kaiserreichs war die des klassischen Griechenlands, den Zwecken eines starken Kaiserreichs angepaßt. Die charakteristische griechische Kunst war die Bildhauerei; und trotz Kriegsschrecken, Fanatismus und sinnloser Gier hat sich in Italien viel mehr als anderswo erhalten. Während der Renaissance war Italien in den schönen Künsten, im Wissen und in der Literatur in der ganzen Welt führend, und man könnte beinahe behaupten, daß fast bis ans Ende des neunzehnten Jahrhunderts ein großer Teil der Literatur des Westens und der größte Teil seiner Kunst, auf direkte oder indirekte Weise von Italien und italienischen Idealen beseelt war.

Man braucht ein ganzes Leben, um sich mit diesen Interessen zu beschäftigen, und man kann wohl verstehen, warum Italien die intellektuellen Kreise anderer Länder schon seit vielen Jahren so sehr bezaubert hat. „Das große Ziel des Reisens", sagt Dr. Samuel Johnson, „ist, das Mittelmeer kennenzulernen." Doch war es zu Dr. Johnson's Zeiten gar nicht leicht, solche Reisen zu unternehmen, als der „Großtürke" mit seinem Fanatismus im Besitz eines so großen Teils der Länder war, die eigentlich hätten europäisch sein sollen — was sie ja auch jahrhundertelang unter Rom gewesen waren. Man mußte damals einen genügend hohen Rang haben und reich genug sein, um diplomatischen Schutzes sicher zu sein, ehe man sich in solche Gebiete wagte, und tatsächlich bedeuteten für die meisten Leute, „die Ufer des Mittelmeers" eigentlich nur Italien. Sizilien und Süditalien wurden wegen Überfallgefahr vermieden, und nur außerordentlich mutige und abenteuerlich veranlagte Männer drangen bis nach Griechenland vor.

Vor dem neunzehnten Jahrhundert war die italienische klassische Kultur — besonders in Neapel und Rom — beinahe die einzige Anziehungskraft für diese wohlhabenden Kulturpilger. Die Grenzen, gesetzt von diesem Geschmack und von der Angst vor den Räubern, können aus den folgenden zwei Episoden beurteilt werden. Ein hochkultivierter englischer Reisender, der viele Monate in Rom verbracht und seine „Eindrücke des Altertums" ausführlich aufgezeichnet hat, bemerkte auf dem Heimweg, daß Venedig „einige Stunden der Überraschung" bot. Vermutlich stammte die Überraschung daher, daß der Verkehr auf Kanälen stattfindet, aber da Venedig keine klassische Stadt ist, hatte der Reisende für ihre Schönheit kein Auge, und für ihre Kunst nur wenig Interesse.

Die andere Episode ist sehr erstaunlich. Angeblich wurden die drei prächtigen griechischen Tempel in Paestum von der gebildeten Welt völlig vergessen, bis sie im achtzehnten Jahrhundert von einer Gruppe abenteuerlicher Fremden „entdeckt" wurden. Diese Zustände werden denjenigen, die heute diese Tempel auf bequeme und schnelle Weise, entweder im Zug oder auf der Autostraße, besuchen, beinahe unglaublich vorkommen; denn sie haben sich in den letzten zweihundert Jahren völlig verändert. Die schwache Regierung „Beider Sizilien" unternahm damals nichts, um die neapolitanischen Camorra, die die reichen Ausländer erpreßten, oder die Räuber, die zwischen Salerno und Pästum, wie überhaupt überall in Süditalien, tätig waren, auszurotten und ihre Macht in Schranken zu halten. Die jungen Damen von damals sollen — ihren Tagebüchern nach — halb auf den Anblick „wirklicher Banditti" gehofft haben, obgleich sie die Wirklichkeit genausowenig freudig wie die erhebliche Wahrscheinlichkeit, sich Malaria zu holen, willkommnet hätten.

Pästum war also gut vor der Welt geschützt. Auch nachdem die Tempel in das moderne Touristengebiet einbegriffen wurden, behauptete sich das Vorurteil gegen Süditalien, und noch um 1930 herum führte die ausgezeichnete Autostraße, die südlich von Neapel verläuft, nur nach Pästum, oder vielmehr wurde sie von da an durch eine sehr viel weniger gute Straße weitergeführt. In früheren Zeiten bis ins neunzehnte Jahrhundert konnte der südliche Teil Italiens von Salerno an und die Insel Sizilien von Fremden nur in bewaffneter Begleitung besucht werden.

Auch als man sich noch auf das Gebiet zwischen den Alpen und dem Golf von Neapel beschränken mußte, war Italien so vielseitig, daß sich eine dauernd wechselnde, internationale Gesellschaft in den Städten aufhielt, besonders in Rom. Die Buntheit Italiens bedeutete, jedenfalls bis zum Anfang des Krieges im Jahre 1939, daß Italien viele friedliche Ausländer beherbergte, die irgendein Thema italienischer Geschichte, Literatur oder Kunst studierten, und dabei zufrieden ihr Leben auf diese Weise hier verbrachten, Bücher schrieben, Bilder malten, oder sich dem Glück hingaben, in einem so schönen Land zu leben. Viele Bücher oder Teile von Büchern sind über die berühmten Leute, die hier gelebt haben oder zu Besuch kamen, geschrieben worden, aber es ist schade, daß niemand im letzten Jahrhundert daran gedacht hat, die Besuche der bescheideneren Gäste aufzuzeichnen, deren Aufenthalt höchstens durch ein paar Ölgemälde, die an den Wänden kleiner Pensionen verbleichen, durch ein vergessenes Reisebuch, oder — noch weniger schmeichelhaft — durch einen niegelesenen Gedichteband in Erinnerung bleibt.

Italien und seine aufeinander folgenden Regierungen haben schon lange ihre Verantwortung als Beschützer der malerischen Städte und der unzähligen Kunstwerke aller Art, die Italien von einer so langen und so fruchtbaren Vergangenheit geerbt hat, erkannt. Wie auch in Spanien, hat sich die Religion als Beschützer erwiesen, und die Kathedralen sowie viele Kirchen sind Museen der Bildhauerei und der Malerei sowohl als heilige Stätten. Man könnte sie tatsächlich die Kunstsammlungen der Armen nennen, da diese nie solche Werke sehen würden. Die Kunstwerke sind zumeist in gutem Zustande erhalten, denn hier gab es ja keine puritanischen oder politischen Zerstörungen, wie sie England und Frankreich erlebt hat, und keine modernen Barbaren, die Stücke von Denkmälern abhauen oder ihr Monogramm in Marmor meißeln. Doch wurde der italienische Schutz seiner eigenen Erbschaft früher ziemlich heftig kritisiert, trotz der großen Geldsummen, die für die Erhaltung ausgegeben wurden. Der zweite Weltkrieg, der sich zerstörend von einem Ende Italiens bis zum anderen wälzte, hat die Last der Verantwortung in gewisser Hinsicht vermindert, ohne jedoch die ganze Wirkung merklich herabzusetzen.

Natürlich kann ein großes, energisches Volk nicht nur in historischen Gebäuden wohnen. Es gibt tatsächlich solche Meisterwerke der Renaissance wie zum Beispiel: Pienza, den Geburtsort Pius' II. und Lecce in Puglien, es wäre jedoch töricht, zu erwarten, daß ganz Italien so wunderbar erhalten sein könnte. In den großen modernen Städten, Mailand, Genua, Neapel, ja selbst in Rom, hat sich die Bevölkerung beträchtlich vermehrt, und viele neue Stadtteile sind entstanden. Genua sieht teilweise ganz amerikanisch aus. Wir brauchen diese Richtung der Entwicklung auch gar nicht zu bedauern, solange die schönen älteren Stadtteile und Gebäude erhalten werden.

Es gab nie einen enthusiastischeren, ja fanatischeren Liebhaber des mittelalterlichen Italien und seiner Kunst als den englischen Kritiker John Ruskin. Es gibt folgende amüsante, wenn auch vielleicht nicht ganz wahre Geschichte über ihn. Nachdem er lange Wochen in alten Bergstädten, Assisi, Perugia, Gubbio, Montepulciano, in sorgsamer Forschung ihrer Kunstgeschichte verbracht hatte, pflegte er plötzlich aufzuhören, mit einem Schnellzug in eine große, moderne Stadt zu fahren, seinen Frack anzuziehen, in einem eleganten Restaurant sein Abendbrot einzunehmen und dann ein Theater oder die Oper zu besuchen, worauf er dann zu seinen Giottos und Peruginos zurückkehrte. Hierin liegt eine wichtige Lehre. Wie erfrischend und anregend wir auch eine Flucht in den unbeschwerten Frieden der Vergangenheit finden — wir können in ihm nicht leben.

Wenn wir uns nun das moderne Italien genau betrachten, finden wir, daß es aus Verwaltungsgründen in Provinzen eingeteilt ist. Einige dieser Provinzen tragen die Namen der alten Freistädte oder Herzogtümer, aber man sollte nicht vergessen, daß sie heute nicht immer dasselbe Gebiet bedecken wie damals, als einige früher bedeutende ihren Namen nur der Hauptstadt geben — wie die von Mailand, Ferrara, Mantua und auch Urbino. Das neue vereinigte Italien ist noch kein Jahrhundert alt, eine kurze Zeit in der Geschichte eines so alten Landes. Erst nach der Niederlage Frankreichs in dem französisch-preußischen Krieg von 1870, wurde Rom zur Hauptstadt des damaligen italienischen Staates, der die Kirchenstaaten in seine Herrschaft miteinbegriff. Vor 1914 beklagten sich viele Leute in Rom — Einheimische sowie Ausländer — über die Verwandlung des kirchlichen Hauptsitzes einer Weltreligion in die Hauptstadt eines modernen Königreiches, heute einer Republik. Aber welche andere Stadt hätte man in Frage ziehen können, trotz des Reichtums und der Handelsmacht Mailands und trotz der Tatsache, daß sie eine Zeitlang die Hauptstadt des römischen Kaiserreiches gewesen war?

Dadurch, daß die Einigung Italiens vor relativ so kurzer Zeit vor sich ging, besteht der lokale Patriotismus und die Eigentümlichkeiten der uralten Freistädte weiter, und das historische Gedächtnis ist noch lebendig. Ich erlebte ein amüsantes kleines Beispiel davon im Jahre 1930, während einer Tour durch Sizilien in einem Wagen mit einer florentinischen Autonummer. Mehr als einmal wurden wir plötzlich mit dem Schrei „Palle! Palle!" begrüßt, dem alten Sammelsignal der Partei Medici. Ich nahm an, daß es spöttisch gemeint wäre, aber mein italienischer Freund sagte, nein, das wäre ein heimwehkranker Florentiner gewesen. In der Tat beschwerten sich in jenen Zeiten die Leute aus den wohlhabenderen, nördlichen Teilen Italiens bitter, über das, was sie die „Roheit" des Südens nannten, und sehnten sich in die Gemütlichkeit ihrer Heimatstädte zurück. Diese Zustände sind daran, sich zu ändern, aber die alten Unterschiede im Volk bestehen weiter, und niemand, der einmal in Italien gelebt hat, würde einen Venezianer für einen Florentiner, oder einen Genuesen für einen Römer halten. In ihren eigenen Augen sind die Einwohner Roms noch „das römische Volk" oder „die Römer", und was die übrige Welt „Römer" nennt, nennen sie würdevoll „die *alten* Römer". Das Gefühl der Unveränderlichkeit und des Stolzes ist eindrucksvoll, und es gibt sogar einen Streit zwischen den beiden Ufern des Tibers, welches das wahre „Rom" ist.

Trotz all diesem lokalen Stolz und Vorurteilen, scheint es nichts von jenem Absonderungsgeist zu geben, den man auf den britischen Inseln und zu einem gewissen Grade im Elsaß, in der Bretagne und sogar, wenn auch sehr milde, in der Provence findet. Alle vernünftigen Italiener sind von der Notwendigkeit und den Vorteilen ihrer Vereinigung überzeugt (wie auch die meisten aller gescheiten Franzosen), aber sie geben die alten Traditionen mit Bedauern auf. Man lese den tönenden, tausend Jahre alten Appell der venezianischen Dogen und man frage sich, ob man von einem Vertreter des Innenministeriums — mag er noch so freundlich und patriotisch sein — sich genauso ergriffen fühlen würde.

Trotz der wichtigen, wirklich entscheidenden Rolle, die Cavour und die Piemontesen in der Befreiung und Vereinigung Italiens spielten, erweckt Piemont einen weit weniger italienischen Eindruck als die übrigen Provinzen. Abgesehen von Turin, das bis 1860 die Hauptstadt des Königreichs Sardinien war, liegt der Reiz der Provinz Piemont größtenteils in der Landschaft am Fuße der Alpen, besonders in dem schönen Aostatal, und in den Bergfesten. Die Provinz Lombardei bringt uns gleich in das geschichtliche Italien, in dem sich die großen herzoglichen Städte Mailand und Mantua befinden — vom Geburtsort Vergils zu d'Annunzios letztem Wohnort — Orte, verbunden durch ihre literarische Vergangenheit; und an den Comer See, den Lago Maggiore, den Gardasee und den Iseosee. Kein Besucher Italiens wird Mailands riesige spätgotische Kathedrale übersehen, die eine der schönsten und größten der Welt ist, oder die große Festung und zugleich Palast der Sforza, die Poldo-Pezzoli Gallerie, oder die Kirche St. Ambrogio, oder Leonardos Abendmahl. Meine persönliche Auswahl fällt auch noch auf Pavia und das in seiner Nähe gelegene große Karthäuser-Kloster mit seinen herrlichen aus der Renaissancezeit stammenden Verzierungen, von den Kreuzgängen bis an das leere Grab Ludovicos und auf Mantua mit seinem fesselnden herzoglichen Palast, dem Palazzo del Té, und die Kirche, wo Mantegna ruht. Giulio Romano arbeitete lange an dem Palast und schuf merkwürdige Fresken, die Riesen darstellen; und sogar Gemälde von Lieblingsrennpferden. Doch wenn man erst anfängt, sich an Einzelheiten in Italien erinnern zu wollen, gibt es kein Ende.

Die stolze Stadt Venedig gibt der Provinz Venedig ihren Namen, und in den Zeiten, in denen das St-Markus-Banner über dem Dom flatterte, interessierte man sich kaum für das rot-weiß-grüne Banner.

Was kann man schon in einem Absatz über Venedig schreiben? — „Oh, was würde ich für eine Stunde mit dem alten blinden Dandolo geben!"? Oder das Gemälde Bellinis Lorenzo Loredans in London? Oder ein paar Zeilen von einem Gedicht, das einmal in dem Witzblatt „Punch" erschien, und ungerufen aus einem Winkel meines Gedächtnisses hervorspringt? Es ist eine Parodie auf Robert Brownings Heimwehgedicht: „Oh, in England zu sein, wenn es Frühling wird!"

„Mein lieber Robert, ich muß es dir sagen —
Unsre Heimat will ich ja nicht anklagen —
Doch wie England für dich,
Hält Venedig für mich
Mein ganzes Glück im April!"

Doch für einen Besuch in Venedig sind ungefähr sechs Wochen genug. Dann fängt man allmählich an, sich nach „dem Grünen und nach Einsamkeit" zu sehnen, um erstaunt zuzusehen, wie Menschen ihr ganzes Leben, nur von Himmel, Wasser und Stein umgeben, verbringen können. Ganz in der Nähe liegen Padua, Vicenza, Verona. In einer privaten Villa vor Vicenza gibt es einige ausgezeichnete Tiepolo-Fresken, und als mir das Privileg zuteil wurde, sie zu sehen, war ich erstaunt, ein Exemplar von James Joyces „Ulysses" im Salon liegen zu sehen!

Das moderne Emilia verbindet Bologna *la grassa*, das herzogliche Ferrara mit seinen Erinnerungen an Ariost und Tasso, Parma und Corregio, Modena, Rimini — wo der Tempel des Malatesta zerstört wurde — und Ravenna, mit seinen Basiliken und unvergleichlich schönen griechischen Mosaiken, wo Dante starb und Byron sein Herz — nicht zum ersten Mal — verlor. Hier denkt man auch an Theodorich, König der Ostgothen, und an Galla Placidia.

Toskana, das Herz und die Seele des dichterischen Italiens; welch ein Wirrwarr glücklicher Erinnerungen schon der Name „Florenz" hervorruft, und dann gibt es ja noch Siena, Pienza, San Gimignano, Pistoia, Prato, Lucca und Pisa. Was für dichterische Phantasie diese Toskaner haben! Ich erinnere mich gut an den Tag, an dem ich meinen bereits verstorbenen Freund Orioli im Auto nach Prato fuhr, um Kalbfleisch zu kaufen, das, wie er mir versicherte, das beste Kalbfleisch in der Welt sei — bis wir dann ein riesiges Ochsengerippe, von irgendeinem Kyklopen in die Hälfte gehackt, vorfanden, mit der Aufschrift: „Vitello Giovanissimo" — neugeborenes Kalb! Wer könnte ein Volk, dessen Phantasie das Leben so verschönert, nicht lieben? Man sollte sich merken, wie die Toskanische — oder Etruskische — Phantasie sogar Florenz verschönert hat und man respektiere den Spirito del Cupolano. Ich erinnere mich an Tage, die man in der Kathedrale von Siena verbrachte, die alten symbolischen Zeichen entziffernd, die in die versteckten Winkel des mächtigen Kirchenschiffes mit seinem Fries von päpstlichen Büsten gemeißelt sind. Das Kirchenschiff, das in dem Plan für die ungeheure Kathedrale ursprünglich als Kreuzschiff gedacht war, mit deren Bau sogar angefangen wurde, als die Pest alles unterbrach. An Lucca und Pisa denke ich zurück.

Wir haben noch nicht einmal die Hälfte Italiens besprochen. Ob der Urbino-Palast noch auf seinem alten Platz steht? Ob es noch den köstlichen muskateller Wein in San Marino gibt? Und wie steht es um Borgo San Sepolcro, und jenen Bildern von Piero della Francesca, und Arezzo? Orvieto — wie wunderbar es ist, den Fiaschetti, die auf den Bahnsteigen verkauft werden, zu entrinnen, herumzusuchen, und endlich nach sechs oder sieben Stufen in ein uraltes Weingeschäft hinunterzusteigen, um dort kühlen echten Orvieto-Weißwein zu trinken. Ein passender Gegensatz zur Fassade der Kathedrale und der Signorelli-Kapelle, ganz zu schweigen von dem mächtigen Brunnen, aus dem die Päpste (mit *diesem* Wein in nächster Nähe!) Wasser schöpften — zweifellos um sich zu kasteien. Mit Recht benutzte man Esel, die das Wasser hinaufschleppten!

Trotzdem sich die Ansichten über Kunst und Leben geändert haben, trotz der Änderungen, die durch sogenannten „Fortschritt" entstanden, bleibt Rom Italiens stärkster Anziehungspunkt. Ein begeisterter, wenn auch nicht gerade phantasiereicher Verehrer drückte sich folgendermaßen aus: „Venedig ist Venedig, aber Rom ist *Rom*." Man versteht, was er meint! Es soll ungefähr 500 Kirchen in Rom geben, von denen die meisten sehr viel Schönes haben, das des Studiums wert wäre.

Der Vatikan und seine Meilen von Galerien ausgefüllt mit Bildwerken, die Museen, das römische Forum, die Tiberbrücken, die Katakomben, die Mosaiken. Es gibt eine erfundene, jedoch symbolisch wahre Anekdote von einem Papste, der einigen vornehmen Besuchern, die eben angekommen waren, Audienz gab, und jeden fragte, wie lange er in Rom bleiben würde. „Drei Tage", sagte einer. „Ah", sagte der Papst, „Sie werden alles in Rom sehen." „Drei Monate", sagte der zweite. „Sie werden viel von Rom sehen." „Drei Jahre", antwortete der dritte. „Sie werden anfangen, Rom kennenzulernen"...

Natürlich wird es immer Menschen geben, die den Golf von Neapel weniger Neapels als der Inseln, der verschütteten römischen Städte Pompeii und Herkulanum, der landschaftlichen Schönheiten wegen, und der Städte entlang der Straße nach Amalfi wegen vorziehen — Castellammare, Sorrento, Positano, Ravello und Amalfi selbst. Diese Gegend bietet einen Teil der schönsten Küstenlandschaft Europas, die sich nur noch mit den beiden Ufern der Meerenge von Messina vergleichen läßt. Abenteuerlich veranlagte Gemüter, denen es nichts ausmacht, wenn der Weg hart und mühselig ist, sollten sich einmal die Gipfel und Täler der Abruzzen und die besuchten etwas südlich von Pästum gelegenen Teile des alten Königreiches Neapel ansehen.

Und dann gibt es noch Sizilien und Sardinien!

Ein altes neapolitanisches Sprichwort lautet, ziemlich drohend: „Neapel sehen, und sterben!" Das ist doch eine harte Strafe dafür, daß man eine schöne Stadt bewundert! Vielleicht dürften wir es unserer Zeit anpassen und sagen: „Italien sehen und wieder kommen und mehr davon sehen!"

R. A.

Turin. A planned town. Piazza Carlo Emanuele II
Turin. Une ville planée. Piazza Carlo Emanuele II
Turin. Eine nach einem Plan gebaute Stadt. Piazza Carlo Emanuele II

Stupinigi. Poplared avenue to the Lalazzina Mauriziana
Stupinigi. Avenue des peupliers menant au Lalazzina Mauriziana
Stupinigi. Die Pappelallee nach Lalazzina Mauriziana

The Limone Valley
La Vallée de Limone
Das Tal von Limone

The Plain of Piedmont
Plaine de Piémont
Piemont

Vercelli. The Duomo of St. Andrea
Verceil. La Cathédrale de S. Andrea
Vercelli. Der S. Andreas Dom

29

Bobbio Pellice. The High Street
Bobbio Pellice. La Rue principale
Bobbio Pellice. Die Hauptstraße

 Sestriere

Susa. The Romanesque Campanile
Suze. Campanile romain
Susa. Der romanische Glockenturm

Aosta. The Campanile of St. Orso
Aoste. Campanile de S. Orso
Aosta. S. Orso Glockenturm

Aosta Valley. Fenis Castle
Vallée d'Aoste. Château de Fenis
Aostatal. Das Fenis Schloß

Monte Cervino
Mont Cervin
Matterhorn

Milan. The Duomo
Milan. La Cathédrale
Mailand. Der Dom

Milan. The Sforza Castle
Milan. Le Château de Sforza
Mailand. Das Sforza Schloß

Bergamo. The Duomo and Colleoni Chapel
Bergame. La Chapelle de Colléoni
Bergamo. Die Colleoni Kapelle

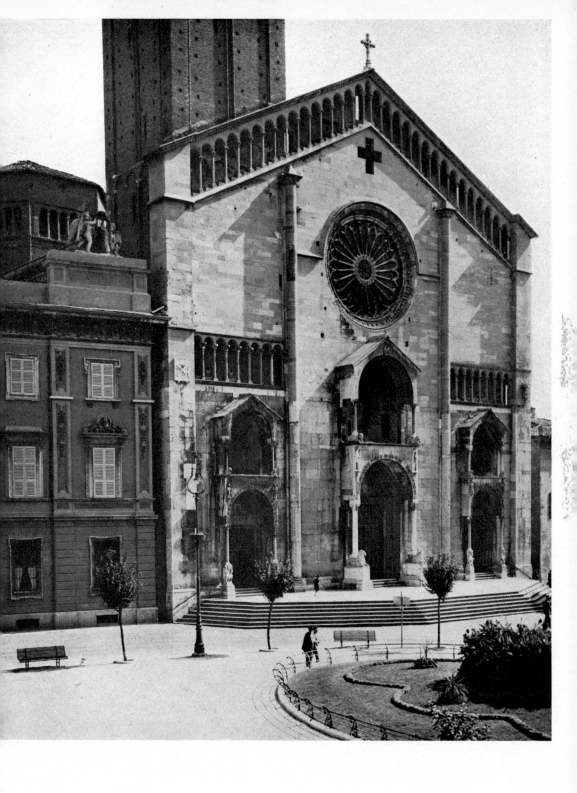

Piacenza. The Duomo
Plaisance. La Cathédrale
Piacenza. Der Dom

Pavia. The Certosa
Pavie. La Certosa
Pavia. Certosa

Cremona. The Torrazzo and the Duomo
Cremona. Le campanile et la cathédrale
Cremona. Der Glockenturm und der Dom

Lake Como. View towards Piona Abbey
Lac de Côme. Vue vers l'abbaye de Piona
Comersee. Blick auf die Piona Abtei

Lake Maggiore. Cannobio
Lac Majeur. Cannobio
Lago Maggiore. Cannobio

Lake Garda. From Salò to Gardone-Riviera
Lac de Garde. De Salò à Gardone-Riviera
Gardasee. Salò bis Gardone-Riviera

Lake Garda. The winding Gardesana Road
Lac de Garde. La Route tournante de Gardésana
Gardasee. Serpentinenstraße nach Gardesana

Lake Iseo. Panorama
Lac d'Iseo. Panorama
Iseosee. Panorama

Lake Iseo. Tavernola Bergamasca
Lac d'Iseo. Tavernola Bergamasca
Iseosee. Tavernola Bergamasca

Canazei. Panorama

Alpe di Siusi. Hyacinths
Alpe di Siusi. Jacinthes
Seiser Alm. Hyazinthen

Scena. Panorama

Merano. Panorama
Méran. Panorama
Meran. Panorama

Lake Toblino
Lac de Toblino
Der Toblino-See

Lake Carezza
Lac Carezza
Der Carersee

Cortina d'Ampezzo. Panorama

The Sella Pass
Le Col de Sella
Der Sella Paß

Trent. The Duomo
Trente. La Cathédrale
Trient. Der Dom

The Pordoi Pass
Le Col de Pordoi
Der Pordoi Paß

Venice. The Piazza of St. Mark's
Venise. La Place St. Marc
Venedig. Markusplatz

 Venice. The Doges' Palace and St. Mark's
Venise. Le Palais des Doges et St. Marc
Venedig. Dogenpalast und Markuskirche

Venice. The Cavalli Palace
Venise. Le Palais des Cavalli
Venedig. Der Cavalli Palast

Venice. The Island of St. George
Venise. L'Ile St. Georges
Venedig. St. Georgs Insel

Vicenza. The Piazza and the Palladio Basilica
Vicence. La Place et la Basilique de Palladio
Vicenza. Platz und Palladio Basilika

Vicenza. The Monte Berico Church
Vicence. L'Église de Monte Berico
Vicenza. Monte Berico Kirche

Montechio Maggiore (Vicenza). The Castles of Romeo and Juliet
Montechio Maggiore (Vicence). Les châteaux de Romeo et de Juliette
Montechio Maggiore (Vicenza). Die Schlösser von Romeo und Julia

Padua. The Basilica of St. Anthony
Padoue. La Basilique St. Antoine
Padua. Die S. Antonio Basilika

Praglia. (Padua). The Abbey
Praglia (Padoue). L'Abbaye
Praglia (Padua). Die Abtei

Euganean Hills
Les Collines d'Euganea
Euganeische Hügel

Verona. The Castel Vecchio and the Scaligero Bridge
Vérone. Le Castel Vecchio et le Pont Scaligero
Verona. Castel Vecchio und die Scaligerobrücke

Trieste. The Church of St. Giusto
Trieste. L'Église S. Giusto
Triest. Die S. Giusto Kirche

Malcesine (Verona). The Scaligero Castle
Malcesine (Vérone). Le Château Scaligero
Malcesine (Verona). Das Schloß Scaligero

Arquà Petrarca

Ravenna. St. Apollinare in Classe, Campanile
Ravenne. Le Campanile de S. Apollinare in Classe
Ravenna. S. Apollinare in Classe, Glockenturm

Bologna. The Asinelli and Garisenda Towers
Bologne. Les Tours d'Asinelli et de Garisenda
Bologna. Die Asinelli und Garisenda Türme

Bologna. The Neptune Fountain, and the Town Hall
Bologne. La Fontaine de Neptune et La Mairie
Bologna. Neptunspringbrunnen und Rathaus

Rimini. The Arch of Augustus
Rimini. L'Arc d'Augustus
Rimini. Das Augustus Tor

Ferrara. The Estense Castle
Ferrare. Le Château d'Estense
Ferrara. Das Schloß Estense

Ferrara. Hemp threshing
Ferrare. Le battement du chenevis
Ferrara. Hanfdreschen

Ferrara. Pomposa Abbey
Ferrare. L'Abbaye Pomposa
Ferrara. Die Pomposa Abtei

Modena. Portal of the Duomo
Modène. Portail de la Cathédrale
Modena. Haupttor des Doms

Parma. The Duomo and Baptistry
Parme. La Cathédrale et le baptistère
Parma. Dom und Taufkapelle

Ravenna. The Mausoleum of Theodoric
Ravenne. Le Mausolée de Théodoric
Ravenna. Theodorichs Mausoleum

From Bocca di Magra to Viareggio
De Bocca di Magra à Viareggio
Bocca di Magra bis Viareggio

The Apuanian Alps
Les Alpes d'Apua
Die Apuanischen Alpen

Viareggio. The pine wood and the Apuanian Alps
Viareggio. La sapinière et les Alpes d'Apua
Viareggio. Kiefernwald und die Apuanischen Alpen

Elba. Procchio

Elba. The 'Mattanza' (Tunny fishing)
Elbe. La pêche du thon
Elba. „Mattanza" (Thunfischerei)

Florence. The Loggia dei Lanzi.
Florence. Loggia dei Lanzi
Florenz. Loggia dei Lanzi

Florence. The Palazzo Vecchio
Florence. Palazzo Vecchio
Florenz. Palazzo Vecchio

Florence. St. Maria del Fiore and Giotto's Campanile
Florence. Ste. Maria del Fiore, et le campanile de Giotto
Florenz. S. Maria del Fiore und Giottos Glockenturm

Florence. Ponte Vecchio
Florenz. Ponte Vecchio

Fiesole. The church of St. Francis
Fiesole. L'Église de St. François
Fiesole. Die Kirche des heiligen Franziskus

Siena. The Cathedral
Sienne. La Cathédrale
Siena. Der Dom

Siena. The Palazzo Publico and the tower
Sienne. Palazzo Publico et la tour
Siena. Der Palazzo Publico mit Turm

Pienza. The Duomo
Pienza. La Cathédrale
Pienza. Der Dom

Volterra. Palazzo Pretorio

Volterra. The 'Mastio'
Volterra. Le „Mastio"
Volterra. „Mastio"

San Gimignano. The Duomo, Piazza and towers
San Gimignano. Place de la cathédrale et les tours
San Gimignano. Dom, Piazza und Türme

Pistoia. The Campanile
Pistoia. Le Campanile
Pistoia. Der Glockenturm

Arezzo. Palazzo Pretorio

Lucca. The Cathedral
Lucques. La Cathédrale
Lucca. Der Dom

Lucca. San Michele
Locques. San Michele

Lucca. Gardens of the Villa Marlia
Lucques. Jardins de la Villa Marlia
Lucca. Gärten der Villa Marlia

Pisa. View from the Aurelia Highway
Pise. Vue de la grand'route d'Aurelia
Pisa. Blick von der Aurelia-Landstraße

Pisa. The leaning tower
Pise. La tour penchante
Pisa. Der schiefe Turm

Pescia. Olive groves
Pescia. Les olivaies
Pescia. Olivenhaine

San Remo. Panorama looking towards Taggia
San Remo. Le panorama vers Taggia
San Remo. Panorama von Taggia

Ligurian coastal road
Route littorale de la Ligurie
Ligurische Küstenstraße

Genoa. The Porta Soprana
Gênes. La Porte Soprana
Genua. Soprana—Tor

Genoa. The Duomo (detail)
Gênes. La Cathédrale (détail)
Genua. Der Dom (Detail)

Portofino. Panorama

Santa Margherita

Rapallo. The bay
Rapallo. La baie
Rapallo. Die Bucht

Manarola

Santa Margherita

Riomaggiore and the Cinque Terre coast
Riomaggiore et la côte de Cinque Terre
Riomaggiore und die Küste von Cinque Terre

Vernazza

Portovenere. The Byron Grotto
Portovenere. La Grotte de Byron
Portovenere. Byron-Grotte

Rome. The Colosseum
Rome. Le Colisée
Rom. Das Kolosseum

Rome. The basilica of St. Peter
Rome. La Basilique St. Pierre
Rom. S. Peter-Basilika

Rome. Ara Coeli
Rom. Ara Coeli

Rome. Castel Sant' Angelo
Rom. Castel Sant' Angelo

Rome. Trajan's Column
Rome. La colonne de Trajan
Rom. Trajans-Säule

Perugia. The Town Hall
Pérouse. La Mairie
Perugia. Das Rathaus

Perugia. Via Ercolano
Pérouse. Via Ercolano

Rome. Trinità dei Monti
Rom. Trinità dei Monti

Rome. Panorama from Trinità dei Monti
Rome. Panorama de Trinità dei Monti
Rom. Panorama von Trinità dei Monti

Rome. The Arch of Constantine
Rome. L'Arc de Constantine
Rom. Constantins-Tor

Rome. The fountain in the Piazza Esedra
Rome. La fontaine de la Piazza Esedra
Rom. Springbrunnen auf der Piazza Esedra

Rome. The church of Santa Maria in Cosmedin
Rome. L'Église de Santa Maria in Cosmedin
Rom. Kirche von Santa Maria in Cosmedin

Tivoli. Villa D'Este

Castelgandolfo. Gardens of the Papal Villa
Castelgandolfo. Jardins de la Villa papale
Castelgandolfo. Gärten der päpstlichen Villa

Montecassino. The rebuilt Abbey
Montecassino. L'Abbaye reconstruite
Montecassino. Die wiederaufgebaute Abtei

Subiaco. The Aniene valley and the convent of Santa Scholastica
Subiaco. La Vallée d'Aniene et le couvent de Santa Scholastica
Subiaco. Das Aniotal und das Nonnenkloster von Santa Scholastica

Rome. The ancient Appian Way
Rome. L'ancienne Via Appia
Rom. Die alte Via Appia

Terracina through the Roman wall
Terracina vu à travers les murs romains
Terracina durch die römischen Mauern gesehen

134

View of the Roman countryside
Vue de la campagne romaine
Eine römische Landschaft

Perugia. Palazzo dei Priori
Pérouse. Palazzo dei Priori

Spoleto. The Duomo
Spolète. La Cathédrale
Spoleto. Der Dom

Spoleto. La Rocca
Spolète. La Rocca

Todi. The Town Hall
Todi. La Mairie
Todi. Das Rathaus

Orvieto. The Duomo
Orvieto. La Cathédrale
Orvieto. Der Dom

Orvieto. Medieval houses
Orvieto. Maisons médiévales
Orvieto. Mittelalterliche Häuser

Viterbo. A medieval street
Viterbo. Une rue médiévale
Viterbo. Eine mittelalterliche Straße

La Verna. Entrance to the sanctuary
La Verna. Entrée de la sanctuaire
La Verna. Eingang zum Heiligtum

Gubbio

Assisi. The Basilica Superiore
Assise. La Basilique Supérieure
Assisi. Die Basilika Superiore

Assisi. Vespers at St. Damiano
Assise. Vêpres à S. Damiano
Assisi. Vesper in S. Damiano

Assisi. Side view of the Basilica Superiore
Assise. La Basilique Supérieure vue du côté
Assisi. Seitenansicht der Basilika Superiore

Ancona. The Cathedral
Ancône. La Cathédrale
Ancona. Der Dom

Urbino. The ducal palace
Urbino. Le palais des Ducs
Urbino. Der herzögliche Palast

Poppi. The Guidi castle
Poppi. Le château des Guidi
Poppi. Das Guidi-Schloß

San Marino
Saint-Marin

Caserta. An avenue in the Villa Reale
Caserta. Une avenue de la Villa Reale
Caserta. Eine Allee in der Villa Reale

Caserta. Diana and Actaeon
Caserta. Diane et Actaeon
Caserta. Diana und Aktäon

Ercolano. The Cervi House
Ercolano. La maison des Cervi
Ercolano. Das Cervihaus

Ercolano. A street
Ercolano. Une rue
Ercolano. Eine Straße

Pompeii. Via dell'Abbondanza
Pompéi. Via dell'Abbondanza
Pompeji. Via dell'Abbondanza

Pompei. The Vettii House
Pompéi. La maison des Vettii
Pompeji. Das Vettihaus

Pozzuoli. Amphitheatre
Pouzzoles. Amphithéâtre
Pozzuoli. Amphitheater

Naples. View from Sant' Antonio
Naples. Vue de Sant' Antonio
Neapel. Blick von Sant' Antonio

Naples. The Angevin Castle
Naples. Le Château Angevin
Neapel. Das Schloß Anjou

Sorrento. Vesuvius from the coastal road
Sorrente. Le Vésuve vu de la route littorale
Sorrento. Der Vesuv von der Küstenstraße gesehen

Ischia. Procida in the background
Ischia. Procida au fond
Ischia. Procida im Hintergrund

Meta di Sorrento. Panorama

Nisida. View from Posillipo
Nisida. Vue de Posillipo
Nisida. Blick von Posillipo

Capri. View from the Villa of Tiberius
Capri. Vue de la Villa de Tibère
Capri. Blick von der Tiberius-Villa

Praiano

Amalfi. The Duomo
Amalfi. La Cathédrale
Amalfi. Der Dom

Amalfi. View from the Albergo Cappuccini
Amalfi. Vue de l'Albergo Cappuccini
Amalfi. Blick vom Albergo Cappuccini

Ravello. The coast from the Villa Rufolo
Ravello. La côte vue de la Villa Rufolo
Ravello. Die Küste von der Villa Rufolo aus gesehen

Atrani

Paestum. The Greek Temple
Paestum. Le Temple grec
Pästum. Der griechische Tempel

Agropoli

L'Aquila. The Church of Sta. Maria di Collemaggio
L'Aquila. L'église de Sta. Maria di Collemaggio
L'Aquila. Kirche von Sta. Maria di Collemaggio

Pescocostanzo. Sixteenth-century houses
Pescocostanzo. Maisons du seizième siècle
Pescocostanzo. Häuser aus dem sechzehnten Jahrhundert

Rural life
La vie champêtre
Landleben

A village fountain
Une fontaine villageoise
Ein Dorfspringbrunnen

Scanno. Panorama

Rocca di Mezzo

The Pescara Valley
La Vallée de Pescara
Das Pescaratal

Taranto. Angevin Castle
Tarante. Château Angevin
Taranto. Das Schloß Anjou

Bari. The Basilica of St. Nicola
Bari. La Basilique St. Nicolas
Bari. Basilika S. Nicola

Troja. The Cathedral
Troja. La Cathédrale
Troja. Der Dom

Castel del Monte. Frederick II's Castle
Castel del Monte. Château de Frédéric II
Castel del Monte. Das Schloß Friedrichs II.

Fasano. The 'trulli'
Fasano. Les «Trulli»
Fasano. Die „Trulli"

Melfi. The Cathedral
Melfi. La Cathédrale
Melfi. Der Dom

Sasso Barisano (Matera)

Matera. The Church of St. John the Baptist
Matera. L'Église de St. Jean Baptiste
Matera. Die Kirche Johannes des Täufers

 Campobasso. Panorama

Capracotta. Panorama

 Scalea. Torre Talso

San Giovanni in Fiore. Local costumes
San Giovanni in Fiore. Costumes régionaux
San Giovanni in Fiore. Ortstrachten

Tagliacozzo. Panorama

San Nicola Arcella. Arcomagno Grotto
San Nicola Arcella. La Grotte d'Arcomagno
San Nicola Arcella. Die Grotte von Arcomagno

Sila Grande. Panorama

Sila Grande. Panorama

Messina. The strait
Messine. Le détroit
Messina. Meerenge

Messina. The Duomo
Messine. La Cathédrale
Messina. Der Dom

Palermo. The Cathedral
Palerme. La Cathédrale
Palermo. Der Dom

Palermo. San Giovanni degli Eremiti
Palerme. San Giovanni degli Eremiti

Palermo. The harbour
Palerme. Le port
Palermo. Der Hafen

Taormina. Etna
Taormina. Ätna

Catania. Etna
Catane. Etna
Catania. Ätna

Taormina. The Greek Theatre
Taormina. Le Théâtre grec
Taormina. Das griechische Theater

Syracuse. The Greek theatre
Syracuse. Le théâtre grec
Syrakus. Das griechische Theater

Syracuse. The Duomo
Syracuse. La Cathédrale
Syrakus. Der Dom

Monreale. The Apse of the Duomo
Monreale. L'abside de la cathédrale
Monreale. Der Dom: Apsis

Monreale. The Cloister
Monreale. Le Cloître
Monreale. Das Kloster

Agrigento. The Temple of the Dioscuri
Agrigente. Le Temple des Dioscuri
Agrigento. Der Dioscurentempel

Cefalù. The Duomo
Cefalù. La Cathédrale
Cefalù. Der Dom

Cefalù from the coastal road
Cefalù de la route littorale
Cefalù von der Küstenstraße aus gesehen

Solunto. Pastoral life
Solunto. La vie pastorale
Solunto. Hirtenleben

Segesta. The Temple
Segesta. Le Temple
Segesta. Der Tempel

Catania. The Duomo
Catane. La Cathédrale
Catania. Der Dom

Cagliari. The Duomo
Cagliari. La Cathédrale
Cagliari. Der Dom

Laerru. Old country church
Laerru. Vieille église champêtre
Laerru. Alte Landkirche

Barumini. The Church
Barumini. L'Église
Barumini. Die Kirche

Silanus. A 'nuraghe' (primitive structure)
Silanus. Un «nuraghe» (bâtiment primitif)
Silanus. „Nuraghe" (Bauwerk aus dem Altertum)

Aggius. Mountain landscape
Aggius. Paysage montagneux
Aggius. Berglandschaft

Sardinian costumes
Costumes de la Sardaigne
Sardinische Trachten

Aggius. The Church
Aggius. L'Église
Aggius. Die Kirche

Bosa. Nuoro

LIST OF ALTERNATIVE PLACE-NAMES
LIEUX CONNUS SOUS DES NOMS DIFFÉRENTS
ORTE, DIE UNTER VERSCHIEDENEN NAMEN BEKANNT SIND

(E) = English / Anglais / Englisch; (F) = Français / French / Französisch; (D) = Deutsch / German / Allemand

Agrigente (F) = Agrigento

Ancône (F) = Ancona

Aoste (F) = Aosta

Assise (F) = Assisi

Ätna (D) = Etna

Bergame (F) = Bergamo

Bologne (F) = Bologna

Catane (F) = Catania

Côme, Lac de (F), Comersee (D) = Lago di Como

Elbe, Ile d' (F) = Elba

Ferrare (F) = Ferrara

Florence (E, F), Florenz (D) = Firenze

Garde, Lac de (F) = Lago di Garda

Gênes (F), Genoa (E), Genua (D) = Genova

Leghorn (E) = Livorno

Ligurie (F), Ligurien (D) = Liguria

Livourne (F) = Livorno

Lucques (F) = Lucca

Mailand (D) = Milano

Majeur, Lac (F) = Lago Maggiore

Meran (D) = Merano

Messine (F) = Messina

Milan (E, F) = Milano

Naples (E, F), Neapel (D) = Napoli

Padoue (F), Padua (E, D) = Padova

Palerme (F) = Palermo

Pästum (D) = Paestum

Pavie (F) = Pavia

Pérouse (F) = Perugia

Piedmont (E), Piémont (F), Piemont (D) = Piemonte

Pise (F) = Pisa

Plaisance (F) = Piacenza

Pompéi (F), Pompeii (E), Pompeji (D) = Pompei

Pouzzoles (F) = Pozzuoli

Ravenne (F) = Ravenna

Rom (D), Rome (E, F) = Roma

Saint-Marin (F) = San Marino

Sienne (F) = Siena

Spolète (F) = Spoleto

Suze (F) = Susa

Syracuse (E, F), Syrakus (D) = Siracusa

Tarent (D), Tarente (F) = Taranto

Triest (D = Trieste

Turin (E, F, D) = Torino

Venedig (D), Venice (E), Venise (F) = Venezia

Verceil (F) = Vercelli

Vérone (F) = Verona

Vicence (F) = Vicenza

INDEX

ACKNOWLEDGEMENTS

Ente Provinciale Turismo, Bergamo. 18

Ente Provinciale Turismo, Ancona. 155

Ente Provinciale Turismo, Cremona (Foto Negri). 22

Ente Provinciale Turismo, Vicenza (Foto Vaienti). 56/58

Ente Provinciale Turismo, Ferrara. 69, 70, 72

Ente Provinciale Turismo, Carrara (Foto Michelino). 78/80

Ente Provinciale Turismo, La Spezia (Foto Zancolli). 117/120 (Foto Servadei). 121

Ente Provinciale Turismo, Pisa. 96, 104, 106

Ente Provinciale Turismo, Lucca. 100/102

Ente Provinciale Turismo, Milano (Foto Stefani). 15

Ente Valorizzazione Isola d'Elba (Foto P. Ridi). 81/82

Azienda Autonoma Turismo, Siena (Foto Grassi). 89/93

Ente Nazionale Italiano di Turismo, Roma. 1/14, 17, 19, 20/21, 23/50, 53, 59/68, 71, 73/77, 83/88, 94/95, 97/99, 103, 105, 107/116, 122/154, 156/240

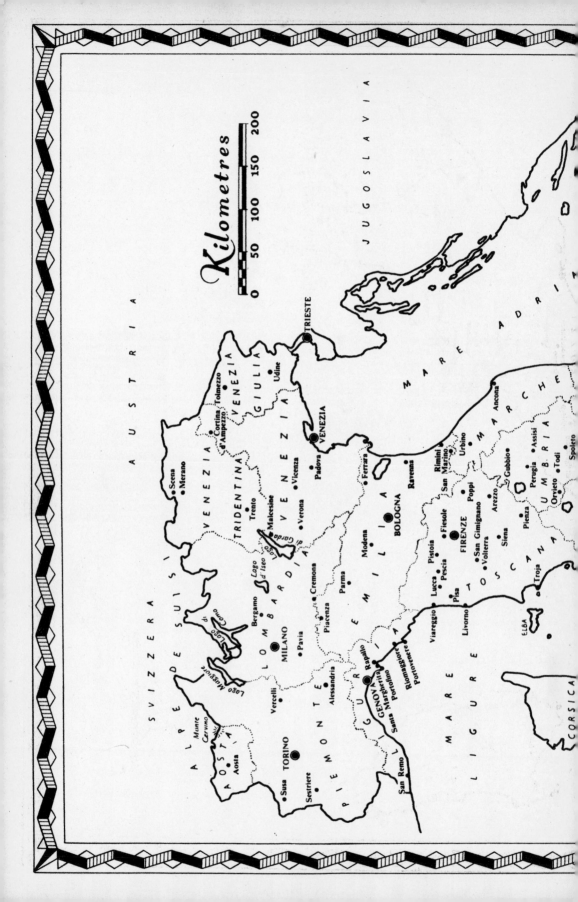